S0-AJD-621

Building the Three Gorges Dam

L. Patricia Kite

LIBRARY
FRANKLIN PIERCE UNIVERSIT
RINDGE, NH 03461

Chicago, Illinois

www.heinemannraintree.com
Visit our website to find out
more information about
Heinemann-Raintree books.

To order:
☎ Phone 888-454-2279
💻 Visit www.heinemannraintree.com
to browse our catalog and order online.

© 2011 Raintree
an imprint of Capstone Global Library, LLC
Chicago, Illinois

All rights reserved. No part of this publication
may be reproduced or transmitted in any form
or by any means, electronic or mechanical,
including photocopying, recording, taping, or
any information storage and retrieval system,
without permission in writing from the publisher.

Edited by Adam Miller, Andrew Farrow, and
Adrian Vigliano
Designed by Philippa Jenkins
Original illustrations © Capstone Global Library
Ltd.
Illustrated by KJA-artists.com
Picture research by Tracy Cummins
Production by Alison Parsons
Originated by Dot Gradations
Printed and bound in China by South China
Printing Company Ltd

14 13 12 11 10
10 9 8 7 6 5 4 3 2 1

**Library of Congress Cataloging-in-Publication
Data**
Kite, L. Patricia.
Building the Three Gorges Dam / L. Patricia
Kite.
p. cm. — (Science Missions)
Includes bibliographical references and index.
ISBN 978-1-4109-3824-4 (hc)
1. San Xia Dam (China) 2. Dams—China—
Yangtze River Gorges. I. Title.
TC558.C52S265 2011
627'.80951212—dc22

2009053325

CUR

Acknowledgments
The author and publishers are grateful to the
following for permission to reproduce copyright
material: Alamy ©Eye Ubiquitous **p.9**; Alamy
©Tina Manley **p.13**; AP Photo/Xinhua, Du Huaju
pp.4&5; AP Photo/Xinhua **p.17**; AP Photo/
Xinhua **p.24**; AP Photo/Xinhua, Zha Chunming
p.25; AP Photo/Xinhua, Li Gang **pp.26&27**; AP
Images/Imaginechina **p.29**; AP Photo/Xinhua,
Du Huaju **p.38**; Corbis ©Long Hongtao/Xinhua
Press **p.7**; Corbis ©REUTERS/China Photo **p.8**;
Corbis ©Swim Ink **p.12**; Corbis ©Huang Wen/
China Features/Sygma **pp.14&15**; Corbis
©Diego Azubel/epa **p.18**; Corbis ©Fritz
Hoffmann **pp.20&21**; Corbis ©Bob Sacha **p.22**;
Corbis ©Liu Liqun **p.28**; Corbis ©Du Huaju/
Xinhua Press **p.32**; Corbis ©Xiaoyang Liu
pp.34&35; Corbis ©Zheng Jiayu/XinHua/Xinhua
Press **p.39**; Corbis ©Zhai Dong Feng/Redlink
p.40; Corbis ©Keren Su **p.41**; Corbis ©Keren Su
p.42; Corbis ©CHINA NEWSPHOTO/Reuters
p.44; Getty Images/China Photos **p.23**; Getty
Images/China Photos **pp.30&31**; Getty Images/
ZOU QING/AFP **p.45**; Getty Images/Tim Graham
pp.46&47; Mary Evans ©Illustrated London
News Ltd **pp.10&11**; Shutterstock ©JingAiping
p.16; Shutterstock ©claudio zaccherini **p.37**;
shutterstock ©Thomas Barrat **pp.50&51**.

Cover photograph of the Three Gorges Dam
reproduced with the permission of Corbis
©Xinhua Press.

The author dedicates this book to Will Brant, a
joyous addition to the family.

The publishers would like to thank Daniel Block
for his invaluable help in the preparation of this
book.

Every effort has been made to contact copyright
holders of any material reproduced in this book.
Any omissions will be rectified in subsequent
printings if notice is given to the publisher.

Disclaimer
All the Internet addresses (URLs) given in this
book were valid at the time of going to press.
However, due to the dynamic nature of the
Internet, some addresses may have changed, or
sites may have changed or ceased to exist since
publication. While the author and publisher
regret any inconvenience this may cause
readers, no responsibility for any such changes
can be accepted by either the author or the
publisher.

CONTENTS

Some words are printed in bold, **like this**. You can find out what they mean by looking in the glossary. You can also look out for them in the **WORD STORE** box at the bottom of each page.

THE
YANGTZE RIVER AND
THREE GORGES

The Three Gorges Dam project, which stretches across the Yangtze River in China, is considered the most expensive, enormous engineering project the world has ever seen. A dam is a barrier built across a waterway to control the water flow. The Three Gorges Dam is also a **hydroelectric** plant. This means it uses the energy of the moving water to create electricity.

Some compare the dam to the historic Great Wall of China in terms of size, labor required, costs, and possible benefits. Others continue to argue that it was, and is, a huge mistake. Its benefits, they say, are overshadowed by non-repairable damage to the environment and local culture, as well as to the natural beauty of the Yangtze River.

This book will discuss the dam's history, the controversy that began with the dam's proposal, and why controversy still continues today. It will also explore how engineers and other people have dealt with many challenges during the building of this enormous and historic dam.

First, let's take a look at the area where the dam was created.

Water rushes through the sluice gates of the Three Gorges Dam. The movement of water through the dam produces huge amounts of electricity, but the dam has caused many problems as well.

The long river

The Yangtze (also spelled Changjiang, and meaning "long river") is one of the world's longest rivers. The only longer rivers are the Nile River in Africa and the Amazon River in South America. The Yangtze originates in the glacial marshlands of the **remote** Tibetan plateau. A plateau is an area of land that is high up and fairly level.

From there the melting glacial waters travel 6,300 kilometers (3,900 miles) through mainland China. Hundreds of smaller rivers and lakes join their waters into the enormous Yangtze.

Along the Yangtze's route are 400 million people, about one-third of China's population. Major **industrial** cities are located along the banks of the Yangtze: Chongqing, Wuhan, Nanjing, and the bustling port city of Shanghai. Leaving Shanghai, the Yangtze reaches the East China Sea.

Known since ancient times as the "Golden Waterway," the Yangtze has been a river where people have lived and worked for thousands of years. It is the most-used passage for ships traveling between inland China and the coast by Shanghai.

A huge river like the Yangtze can be very different along its route. This section is scenic and calm, but other areas of the river can be wild!

WORD STORE   **erosion** natural wearing away of soil or rock
industrial related to processing materials and making goods

DRAGON RIVER

The Yangtze River has sometimes been called China's "Dragon River" because its shape looks like a dragon. Look at the map below and imagine that the dragon's tail is at Chongqing, and the dragon's mouth is at Shanghai.

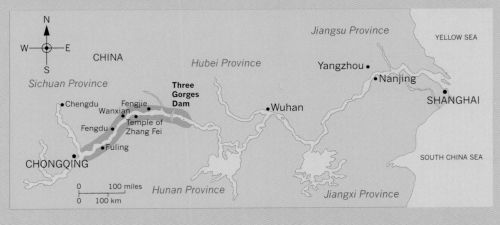

The river constantly removes material from the area surrounding it and deposits it in other places. Material like this that a river carries is often called **silt**. Sometimes the Yangtze carries up to 500 million tons of silt a year. This silt is deposited along the shoreline. **Erosion** along the Yangtze takes away soil from the river's shoreline. So, deposited silt renews the soil that is lost. But this can also cause problems.

While the Yangtze is calm in some areas, sometimes it can become very dangerous. With summer heat and wind, the melting snow and glaciers in the faraway Tibetan plateau start a huge amount of water moving that can become a flood. Rainstorms often happen along with the flooding.

Before the dam was built, the water would rise a little in the wide Yangtze riverbank areas. But in the narrow mountain area called the Three Gorges, a lot of water had to travel through a very limited space. Where the Yangtze traveled through limestone cliffs standing 914 meters (2,999 feet) high, some of the spaces were so narrow and steep it was said sunlight never reached the water.

The Three Gorges

The Three Gorges mountain area got its name because of the unique formations along the Yangtze River. A gorge is a deep, narrow passageway with steep, rocky sides, enclosed between two mountains. The Three Gorges on the Yangtze are named Qutang, Wu, and Xiling.

Qutang

The shortest area, at 8 kilometers (5 miles) long, is Qutang Gorge. It is also the narrowest of the gorges, at only 150 meters (500 feet) wide.

Qutang Gorge once contained many **relics** of ancient civilizations. Boat-shaped cedar coffins from the Ba people, who left the area more than 1,600 years ago, were discovered in caves and on cliffs. Only a few remain. Other ancient sites later covered by rising waters from the dam project include Meng Liang's Staircase, the Chalk Wall, and much of the Ancient Pathway used by human boat-haulers (see box).

Ancient wooden coffins like these existed as historical sites from past civilizations. Many of these sites have now been swallowed by water from the dam project.

WORD STORE   **relic** remains of an object from an earlier time

Wu

The city of Wushan is at the entrance to Wu Gorge. This gorge is 40 kilometers (25 miles) long. Wu Gorge is especially noted for its 12 peaks, which are thought to resemble animals and people. Goddess Peak is a beautiful pillar of white stone resembling a standing maiden.

Xiling

The last and deepest of the Three Gorges is Xiling Gorge. It is also the longest at 76 kilometers (47 miles). Around Xiling Gorge, the cliffs rise to 1,219 meters (4,000 feet) high. This was once considered the most dangerous of the gorge passages.

One of the 12 peaks of Wu Gorge.

Rain and floods

Before the dam project, Three Gorges floodwaters could rise 18 meters (60 feet) in a single day. If the rain continued, water could rise as much as 40 meters (130 feet) higher. When this happened, the water was not only higher—it also became a lot rougher. The Three Gorges area had rapids, whirlpools, dangerous currents, and rock falls.

DANGEROUS WATERS

Traveling through the Three Gorges often used to mean tempting death, especially in rough weather. Small boats could be smashed against the nearby rocks. To get junks (large, flat-bottomed ships) to go upstream against the strong water current rushing downstream, men called "trackers" were employed to pull, or haul, the boats. Tracker teams had to walk on narrow paths cut into the slippery cliffs surrounding the Three Gorges area. It was extremely dangerous work.

A flooded market near the Yangtze in 1931.

WHY BUILD A DAM ACROSS THE YANGTZE RIVER?

But why build a dam across the Yangtze River? The leader Sun Yat-sen, widely regarded as the "National Father of Modern China," proposed the Three Gorges Dam back in 1919. He believed that tremendous economic benefits would result. "Go up from Yichang to the gorges, rapids, and rocks," he wrote. "Improve the upper part of the river and resist the water with the gate, so that ships can go against water following and the hydropower [**hydroelectric** power] can be used."

But due to China's political and economic conditions at the time, Sun Yat-sen's idea for a dam did not move forward at the time.

In 1931, **dikes** holding back the river failed. Summer floods along the Yangtze caused the deaths of 145,000 people. Men, women, and children, along with their pets and farm animals were swept downstream by raging waters. People were buried alive under mudslides.

Two million homes, many made of dried mud, bamboo, and woven straw, were swept into the swirling waters. Vast amounts of farmland were washed away. Without farm crops, and without animals for food and labor, people starved. Combined with the lack of adequate shelter and a contaminated water supply, often-deadly diseases such as cholera and typhus were spread by the floodwaters.

More floods

In 1935 there was another major Yangtze River flood caused by melting glacial waters and heavy rains. This time 142,000 people died, and even more land were flooded.

Again, in 1954, a series of Yangtze River floods caused the deaths of about 33,000 people. This caused the Chinese government to make flood prevention on the Yangtze River a high priority. Mao Zedong, leader of the Chinese Communist Party, declared, "We must still be prepared to do battle against, and overcome, similarly severe floods that may occur in the future."

敬祝我们伟大的领袖毛主席万寿无疆！

A poster of Mao Zedong from 1967. Though he died in 1976, he remains one of the most interesting, and controversial, figures in Chinese history.

Reasons for a dam

These disastrous floods caused people to begin rethinking the idea of building a huge dam by the Three Gorges mountain area. There were four especially important reasons for the dam concept.

1. Flood control
Flooding had to be controlled. The Chinese knew that a major Yangtze flood would occur at least once every 10 years. The huge floods of 1931, 1935, and 1954 had made people even more aware of how destructive the Yangtze could be.

2. Shipping
A safe shipping route was desperately needed. Ships traveling between Chongqing, a major **industrial** city, and the Shanghai coast needed a good route for shipping. A dam would help to provide this route.

WORD STORE   rural country

3. Replacing coal

A substitute for coal had to be found. Coal was burned for fuel everywhere in China, from industrial boilers to home stoves. Many miners died each year digging up the coal. Coal shortages forced people to cut back their electricity use. The country's transportation system creaked under the burden of distributing coal across the country.

To make matters worse, burning the coal turned the air into a massive brown cloud, which was even found to be visible from space. The air pollution from coal was making huge numbers of Chinese people sick with respiratory (breathing-related) problems. A new energy source was desperately needed.

4. Creating hydroelectric power

China urgently needed electricity for its booming economy. In the early 1980s, its population grew larger than a billion people and is still growing today. In the summer, many cities and **rural** areas had power shortages. This slowed down economic expansion.

Some dams are built simply for issues like river flow, navigation improvement, and flood control. But some dams, like the Three Gorges Dam, are also constructed to produce hydroelectric power. Hydroelectric power is a good substitute for coal burning.

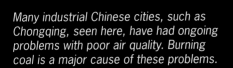

Many industrial Chinese cities, such as Chongqing, seen here, have had ongoing problems with poor air quality. Burning coal is a major cause of these problems.

The Gezhouba Dam in 1997, nearly a decade after it was completed.

PLANNING THE
THREE
GORGES DAM

Mao Zedong's enthusiasm, along with that of **Premier** Zhou Enlai, started the December 1970 construction of a dam on the Yangtze River, just east of the Sichuan Basin border. But this was not the Three Gorges Dam. This was the Gezhouba Dam.

It was originally hoped the Gezhouba Dam would make it unnecessary to build a much larger and more complex dam near the Three Gorges. However, there were numerous problems in design and construction. By 1972 construction of the Gezhouba Dam was suspended. It restarted in 1974, even though the chief commander of the project opposed it. He said China already had the technology to go ahead with a larger dam in the Three Gorges area.

After 18 years, the Gezhouba Dam was finally completed in 1988. At the time, it was the largest dam in China. It is 70 meters (230 feet) high and 2.6 kilometers (1.6 miles) wide. The Three Gorges Dam is located about 38 kilometers (24 miles) from the Gezhouba Dam.

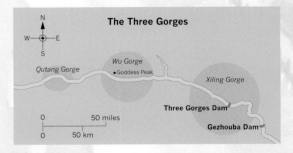

The Three Gorges

N
W—E
S

Qutang Gorge
Wu Gorge
• Goddess Peak
Xiling Gorge
Three Gorges Dam
Gezhouba Dam

0   50 miles
0   50 km

Arguments and delays

Not everyone agreed that another dam was necessary. In addition to protests about the costs, many people felt the money could be better spent elsewhere, such as on education and health services. But Li Peng, the main engineer on the project, said, "The damming of the Yangtze is of great political and economic significance. It proves to the whole world the Chinese people's capability of building the world's first-rate **hydroelectric** project."

Even though a final design was officially due in 1980, plans for the Three Gorges Dam were delayed, due to the huge size of the project. Finally, in 1983 China's **State Council** approved plans for a 170-meter- (491-foot-) high dam. Prompt preparations were made for the dam's construction. This included the building of roads, harbors, and power-supply facilities.

However, just a year later, some engineers suggested that the proposed dam's size would cause disastrous **sedimentation** problems for the large city of Chongqing. At the same time, difficulties getting ships through the Three Gorges area were holding back Chongqing's expansion, and the dam would help to solve this problem.

Plans were changed to make the dam slightly higher. Supporters of the dam argued that this would make the dam more effective in preventing floods, cause less sedimentation, and create more power.

After looking at 16 sites, Sandouping, along the Yangtze River, was chosen for the dam. This site had many advantages. Its rock base would form a good foundation bed for the dam. Also, earthquakes in that area were not strong and did not occur often.

WORD STORE   **hydroelectric** electricity produced by moving water
sediment particles that drop to the bottom of a liquid

It took a civil engineer, Li Peng, to get the Three Gorges Dam project moving. Li Peng was orphaned at age three. He became the adopted son of Premier Zhou Enlai, a strong supporter of Mao Zedong. Li Peng studied at the Moscow Power Engineering Institute, majoring in hydroelectric engineering. In 1987 he became premier of the People's Republic of China, a position he held until 1998. While premier, Li Peng started and continued monitoring what he considers his life's work, the Three Gorges Dam.

At the chosen dam site, Li Peng gave the order to begin blocking the Yangtze so that dam construction could start.

This image of the Yangtze near Chongqing shows high levels of sedimentation, which is why the water appears brown.

WORD STORE   **State Council** one of three main areas of China's government

A farmer makes use of rich farmland along the Yangtze in 2007. This area was eventually flooded to become part of the Three Gorges Dam reservoir. Many people have criticized things caused by the dam's construction, such as massive relocations and the loss of fertile farmland.

WORD STORE   **NPC** one of three main areas of China's government

Problems and complications

Opposition to the Three Gorges Dam within China began increasing. In 1986 China, seeking funding and international support, requested that companies in the United States and Canada offer their opinions about the dam. Initially these groups gave their support, and recommended a 185-meter (607-foot) version of the dam. But, after pressure from environmental groups, much support for the dam was withdrawn.

China's leaders continued to debate the details of the plan. One of several major problems encountered was the relocation of at least 1.3 million people. These people lived in areas that would be flooded by the new dam **reservoir**, the place where the water is collected and stored for use.

New businesses were designed, hoping to provide employment for people facing relocation. A few of these businesses would eventually succeed, such as a cosmetics factory and a silk factory. Other projects were failures, often due to miscalculations about economic needs or transportation problems. (See pages 46 to 49 for more about relocation.)

In 1986 the Chinese People's Political Consultative Conference (CPPCC), a political advisory body, issued a report opposing the construction of the Three Gorges Dam. Among the concerns in the report were flood control and possible problems due to sedimentation.

In 1989 a Canadian study concluded that the Three Gorges Dam was environmentally, economically, and technically possible. Now it looked like China's **National People's Congress (NPC)** would go ahead with plans to build the dam. But only a few months later, the NPC vote was postponed. It appeared that work would not begin on the dam for at least five years.

But, just a year later, Premier Li Peng insisted on a commission to review the Three Gorges project once again. In 1992, a plan for a 185-meter (607-foot) dam received the go-ahead. This was 73 years after Sun Yat-sen first said a Yangtze dam was necessary. The NPC approved the construction of the Three Gorges Dam by a vote of 1,767 people in favor, 177 opposed, and 644 not voting. This was an unusual display of what might be considered public opposition to a government plan.

About 50,000 state-employed Gezhouba Dam workers had been waiting to hear if the project would continue. They had been paid only 70 percent of their salaries for five years, so the project's approval was joyful news for them. They had been living in poverty, yet forbidden to move on to other work while the Three Gorges Dam project was debated.

CONSTRUCTION

At last, construction could begin on the Three Gorges Dam. But before anything could be done, there had to be a way to get tons of materials and thousands of workers to the mountainous dam site.

A new four-lane highway, the Three Gorges Project Expressway, was cut through the mountains. Along this expressway there eventually would be 34 bridges and 5 double-lane tunnels, including a 3.6-kilometer (2.2-mile) single-lane tunnel—the longest in China. In addition, the 899-meter (2,950-foot) Xiling Yangtze Bridge, was built at Sandouping for access to the right side of the dam.

STAGE ONE

In 1994, the first stage of work began. A dam could not be built until the mighty Yangtze River had been diverted, which meant creating a new path for it. Workers created a **diversion channel** for the river waters. They used dump trucks and giant drills that cut through granite. The river was diverted into a long canal. The normal Yangtze water pathway was blocked at the dam site.

In November 1997 more than 4,000 giant loading trucks poured tons of rock and gravel to complete the barrier closure. When the river finally moved into the diversion channel, fireworks went off. Ships' horns blared. Thousands of spectators cheered.

A local woman stands above the Three Gorges Dam site, during its early years of construction.

" Technology is being challenged and stretched to the limit as never before to face a variety of engineering challenges in the construction of the Three Gorges Dam project. "

Wafeek S. Wahby,
Journal of Technology
Studies, 2000

Cofferdams

To allow workers to construct dam supports, make repairs, or do other types of work in a dry environment, the first **cofferdams** were created at the riverbed site. Cofferdams are temporary, watertight walls used in construction projects in areas that are normally underwater. The water is pumped out of the walled areas, allowing workers to proceed in a dry environment. The cofferdams were a massive 580 meters (1,903 feet) long and 140 meters (459 feet) high.

Forced out

Already thousands of Sandouping peasants had left their homes for new villages and factory jobs. By 1995 the area was filled with steel and iron bridges, concrete walls, gates, huge holes in the ground, and piles of dirt. Red and yellow bulldozers moved back and forth.

On dry ground, a worker stands beside one of the Three Gorges cofferdams.

WORD STORE   **cofferdam** temporary, watertight wall

The tiny town of Dachang was one of the few remaining communities that dated all the way back to the period known as the Ming dynasty (1368–1644). For more than 1,700 years, it was a quiet place for families and their respected ancestors. Because it was so **remote** within the Three Gorges Mountains, the town had changed very little over its history. There were ancient city gates, stone roads, and houses. Because of its historic background, in 2003 the Chinese **Relics** Protection Department (CRP) decided to attempt to save at least some of it from the future flooding of the Three Gorges **reservoir**. "This will be a magnificent feat in the history of ancient building protection," said a CRP official.

Thirty-eight historic houses were selected to be saved. Workers carefully marked, then took apart, bricks, tiles, and pillars. The materials were brought to a new, safer site 5 kilometers (3 miles) away and the buildings were reconstructed. "We will try our best to maintain the original look of the town," said a CRP official. But the 10,000 people who lived in Dachang had no choice but to leave their town and move elsewhere. The photo below shows a part of Dachang that was eventually destroyed by the reservoir.

Another flood

In 1998 there was a huge flood along the Yangtze River. Five million houses were destroyed. Huge areas of farmland went underwater. Thirteen million people had to be evacuated, or moved to another area. The death toll was at least 1,000 lives. The economic loss was $12.5 billion. The difficulties that resulted delayed some of the dam construction. But the Chinese government was even more determined to complete the Three Gorges Dam.

The town of Wuhan during the 1998 Yangtze flooding. Many people built makeshift boats to go about their daily business.

STAGE TWO

From 1998 to 2003, stage two of the project was accomplished. More temporary cofferdams were constructed, allowing workers to continue their jobs in a dry environment. Many important projects were completed. For example, workers completed the electricity station facility on the left bank and installed machinery. During this second stage, river water continued flowing through the diversion channel. Ships used either the diversion channel or a temporary ship **lock**.

WORD STORE   **capacity** the total amount that something can contain
lock system that moves boats through a dam

As the dam walls grew higher, the blocked waters behind the walls rose about 5 meters (16 feet) per day. In order to lower construction costs, project officials changed the date for full reservoir filling. The reservoir was supposed to take ten years to fill up completely. Officials ordered it to be done in six years. In response, 53 engineers asked for a delay. They wanted to make certain that a faster filling was safe, due to possible **sedimentation** problems.

The concern was that sedimentation could possibly block the dam's **sluice** gates, which could cause dam failure. (See page 5 for a photo of the sluice gates.) Sediment buildup behind the dam and throughout the reservoir would affect the overall reservoir storage **capacity**. The lower the storage capacity, the lower the amounts of floodwater control.

Despite the engineering request for a delay, construction continued. By 2003 the blocked waters in the reservoir rose to the second-stage goal of 156 meters (511 feet). The dam could now start to generate electricity. The reservoir created by the dam walls would eventually extend 579 kilometers (360 miles) upriver to Chongqing.

As the reservoir filled up, some cultural and historic relics were moved to higher ground. But there was not enough time or money for full protection. Many valuable cultural relics were unearthed during the construction process. This offered antique dealers and thieves great opportunities to steal things.

A building is blown up to make way for the filling of the reservoir.

THE
LOCK SYSTEM

As dam construction progressed, one of the major challenges was finding a way for large ships to deal with the 185-meter (607-foot) height of the dam as they traveled up and down the Yangtze River. Cargo ships weighing up to 10,000 tons had to be somehow accommodated. In addition, the Chinese government, with business in mind, required that a minimum of 5,000 ships per year be able to cross the new dam.

Engineers eventually designed a two-lane, five-step **lock** system. A lock system is somewhat like an enormous series of elevators that move things using water levels instead of pulleys. The lock system's purpose is to get ships from one side of the dam to the other. Each Three Gorges Dam lock is 280 meters (918 feet) long and 35 meters (114 feet) wide. Ships must be moved 113 meters (370 feet) down to get from the **reservoir** side of the dam to the river. But the lock system can move ships up as well as down.

To create space for the multiple lock chambers, workers had to blast enormous amounts of granite from the sides of the Yangtze River.

To the right you can see a large ship leaving the bottom lock chamber. Above it you can see the five chambers of the system the ship was lowered through.

Locks and lifts

A ship entering a lock would be moved up, or down, about 37 meters (120 feet) at a time in a series of five steps. This would be enough to carry it across the dam. A large ship might take about three to four hours to get through the five lock chambers.

Construction of the two-way, five-story, five-step lock, the largest in the world, took nine years, at a cost of almost $747 million. It went into trial operation in 2003, when the Three Gorges reservoir held enough water.

Not all ships crossing the new dam are enormous. A relatively small ship lift was constructed just for smaller business or tourist ships, so they wouldn't have to wait in line for the large lock. Its design was altered several times before completion in 2009. The ship lift is a container that is 19 meters (390 feet) long and 34 meters (110 feet) wide. Once a ship moves into the container, it is taken directly up to its river goal in one elevator movement. It takes about 40 minutes to be lifted.

To meet deadlines, thousands of workers had to pour concrete at a frantic pace. This required an extensive and complex system for transporting enormous quantities of concrete from the mixing plants to the dam. The equipment, from a U.S. supplier, consisted of about 8 kilometers (5 miles) of fast, movable, and rotating conveyor devices.

Constructing the lock system was another huge piece of the dam project.

The Zhang Fei Temple was in the reservoir's path. To protect it from disappearing, experts began work to relocate it.

The Zhang Fei Temple dates back to the Chinese Three Kingdoms period (220–280 CE). Zhang Fei was a brave and loyal warrior. This temple dedicated to him had elegant pavilions and ancient inscriptions, or carvings. Inside the temple were more than 600 beautiful sculptures of historic figures, as well as ancient Chinese woodcarvings.

To prepare for relocation, experts took tens of thousands of color photos. They took apart the ancient temple piece by piece. Every part that was removed from the original temple was numbered, wrapped in cloth, and loaded onto trucks. The relocation team moved not only pieces of the temple, but also plants, railings, rocks, and stone stairs.

The trucks transferred the items to a gigantic boat called a ferry. The ferry took the pieces of the temple to a new site in Bangshang Yuanzi, a town about 32 kilometers (20 miles) upstream on the Yangtze River.

The Zhang Fei Temple after being relocated and rebuilt.

GENERATING POWER

Various problems emerged during the dam building. Expensive repair work to fix large cracks on the dam's concrete exterior had not been completely successful. Inspectors found that some of the repaired vertical cracks on the dam had reopened. Claims were made that contractors (groups paid to do the work) skimped on equipment and materials. There were several well-publicized accidents, including a bridge collapse.

The government ordered some of the dam's infrastructure to be destroyed and redone. A chief engineer emphasized that there was still a long way to go as they entered the third and final phase of dam construction. The goal had been to build a first-class dam, rather than one with 10-meter- (32-foot-) long cracks.

By the end of stage three (2004–2009), the water level behind the dam had risen to its final 175-meter (574-foot) level. The **reservoir** was capable of storing 5 trillion gallons of water. It was ready to generate full power.

The **cofferdams** were no longer needed. The last cofferdam was blown up in June 2006. The demolition took only about 12 seconds, with explosives powerful enough to topple down 400 10-story buildings. The explosions unleashed water into the **hydroelectric** facility.

葛洲坝集 CGGC 围堰爆破圆满成功

A cofferdam being blown up in 2006. Removing the cofferdams allowed for the dam's electricity production to begin.

A lot of power

During this third and final construction stage, the power station on the left bank began working. The permanent ship **lock** system was available for use. The **diversion channel** was no longer needed for navigation. The dam sections and the electricity station on the right riverbank were completed. All machinery was installed.

On October 30, 2008, the 26th hydro-**turbine generator** was brought into action. This meant that all of the planned project parts were completed. Each of these main generators weighs about 6,000 tons. They will generate an estimated 84.7 billion **kilowatt** hours per year. This is equal to the electricity produced by 18 nuclear power plants. The goal is that the dam will be able to supply 10 percent of China's electricity needs.

The completed Three Gorges Dam project will contain 32 main generators. Each will have a **capacity** of 700 megawatts. The six additional generators in the underground power plant are not expected to become fully operational until 2011. The total electricity-generating capacity of the dam will then reach 22,500 megawatts.

Inside one of the enormous power stations on the right bank of the dam.

WORD STORE **diversion channel** area where a river is sent while a dam is built
generator electric motor with magnets and wires

PRODUCING ELECTRICITY

WHAT IS A WATT?

A watt is a unit of power. A typical household incandescent lightbulb uses electrical energy at a rate of 25 to 100 watts. A kilowatt is equal to 1,000 watts. A megawatt is equal to one million watts.

HOW DOES HYDROELECTRIC POWER WORK?

Hydroelectric power is produced as water moves through a dam and into the river below. Inside the powerhouse, generators are connected on top of propeller-like turbines. Water falls on a turbine, causing it to turn. A generator is a large electric motor containing magnets and wires. As water turns the turbine, the components of the generator turn too, and this produces electricity. Electricity is usually produced by turning turbines. Nuclear and coal power plants create heat to make steam, which turns turbines. Dams use the natural movement of a river to do the same thing.

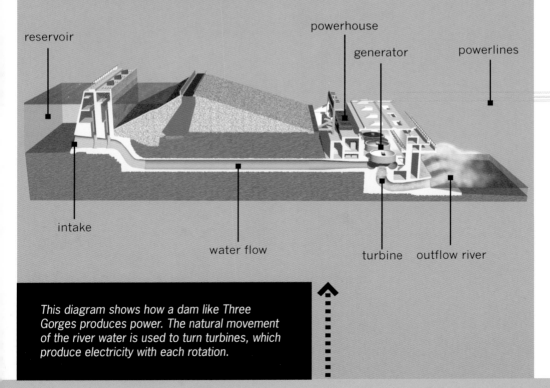

reservoir

powerhouse

generator

powerlines

intake

water flow

turbine

outflow river

This diagram shows how a dam like Three Gorges produces power. The natural movement of the river water is used to turn turbines, which produce electricity with each rotation.

WORD STORE   **kilowatt** unit of power equal to 1,000 watts
turbine piece of a dam that moves to turn a generator

BENEFITS
AND
PROBLEMS

Supporters of the Three Gorges Dam project believe that the benefits far outweigh the disadvantages. But others disagree. Let's begin by taking a look at the project's benefits.

The dam was designed to prevent the very severe flooding that occurred along the Yangtze River about every 10 years. Its construction should also control other major floods. Flooding has claimed more than one million lives in the last 100 years.

Millions of people live downstream from the dam. Many large, important cities like Wuhan, Nanjing, and Shanghai are next to the river. If a major or "super" flood occurs, the dam is expected to make the effect less harmful. The dam's **reservoir** is expected to reduce the severe flooding of the Yangtze by 90 percent.

How will it do this? The water level in the reservoir can be adjusted. As the rainy season approaches, additional storage **capacity** is needed. To accomplish this, the reservoir water can be lowered to the flood-control level of 145 meters (476 feet) high. This enables the reservoir to accept and store rain and possible floodwaters.

When incoming river water or rain causes the reservoir to reach its maximum of 175 meters (574 feet) high, the water will be released in a safe, controlled way. The reservoir waters will then again be lowered to 145 meters (475 feet) high, as needed. During the dry season, or a **drought**, water flows can be increased to meet power demand. The flood-prevention concept was tested in 2009, when the largest rainfall in five years occurred. The dam succeeded in controlling the raging waters within the Three Gorges.

Power generation

With rapid **industrialization** and huge economic growth, China's electricity needs are enormous. The **hydroelectric** power generated by the Three Gorges Dam is estimated to be about 84.6 billion **kilowatt** hours every year. Supporters of the dam argue that this will be enough electricity to offset China's annual consumption of 50 million tons of coal.

The Three Gorges Dam is the biggest hydroelectric producer in the world. Its output should produce about 10 percent of China's electricity needs. Supporters hope that the dam will play an important role in the further development of China's economy and the reduction of environmental pollution.

Air and water

As mentioned above, the Three Gorges Dam should reduce coal consumption by millions of tons per year. Switching to hydroelectric power will also prevent millions of tons of greenhouse gases from being released into the atmosphere, by reducing the need for coal power plants. The release of millions of tons of sulfur dioxide and nitrogen oxides, both contributing to acid rain, will also be prevented. In addition there will be much less dust and other discharge from coal-powered plants that would be needed to provide the same amount of energy.

Since the reservoir filled, the Three Gorges Dam has supplied a lot of freshwater to downstream cities and farms during the dry season. This has helped to ease some of the effects of drought.

WORD STORE   **drought** shortage of water caused by unusually low rainfall

Chinese cities like Shanghai are ultra-modern symbols of the country's explosive economic growth. But huge power demands have come along with this growth and development.

WORD STORE   **industrialization**   the process of developing industries

Navigation improvement

The Three Gorges Dam and reservoir improves the ability of people to navigate, or travel on, the Yangtze River. Now there is a long reservoir of calm, deep water. Strong currents and obstacles such as rocks and sandbars have been eliminated. The shipping lanes are wider.

The Three Gorges Dam allows 10,000-ton ships to travel easily to Chongqing. The previous 10 million tons per year of materials will eventually expand to 50 million tons. While the number of ships and cargo will increase, the costs for this increase will decrease by about 35 percent. Some people have even argued that Chongqing will eventually become the largest seaport in the world.

New forests

The forests along the Yangtze River have always been harvested to meet people's needs. But with increasing numbers of people, forested areas were removed so living areas could be opened up. As people became wealthier, traditional woven straw, dried mud, or bamboo homes lasting a few years were replaced with well-constructed wood homes. As factories multiplied, so did the need for wood products, including furniture, floors, heavy shipping containers, paper bags, and computer paper.

Within the last 50 years, local forests have declined by over 50 percent. Removing thousands of mature trees also removed their land-stabilizing root systems. Landslides have occurred that have destroyed entire villages and valuable crop-growing areas.

A local man fishes below the dam. Debate continues on how the dam will affect people's lives.

Recognizing the need to restore these root systems and control **erosion**, the Chinese government has proposed a $108 million reforestation plan within the Three Gorges area. The new forests will eventually fill an area above the reservoir. This does, however, remove even more of the disappearing farmland by the Yangtze River.

Wastewater

In 2001 $2.55 billion was spent on cleanup projects. Polluting factories have been closed or required to update their factories to be cleaner. In 2001 the first modern **sewage**-treatment plant was put into place in Chongqing. By 2007 about 65 percent of the Yangtze wastewater was being treated before being dumped in the Three Gorges Dam reservoir. Currently about 18 wastewater plants have been constructed. They are treating more than 600,000 tons of sewage daily. In addition, 101 sewage treatment plants are planned in **rural** areas.

Ships passing through the lock system. Supporters of the dam argue that it has allowed for important new developments in water treatment in the Three Gorges area.

More improvements

Supporters argue that the raising and lowering of the reservoir water should handle **silt** control. When the flow is high, **sediment** will be flushed out. Chinese engineers have stated that they understand silting. They say that it has been taken into account, using the best knowledge from around the world. There are silt-prevention **dikes** and silt-clearing **sluices**.

Yichang, the nearest city to the Three Gorges Dam, has added four new trains linking it with Shanghai and Guangzhou. There is a new international airport based in Yichang. Supporters of the dam argue that these improvements would not have happened without it.

Now that the dam is complete, Three Gorges tourism is an increasingly big business. In the past, people came to the area to see the hillside temples carved into towering cliffs, picturesque Ba boats, and tiny ancient towns. Now they come to see the dam, as well as the Yangtze River and the changed Three Gorges Mountains.

A visitor center beside the dam. China hopes that tourism will increase in the Three Gorges area.

WORD STORE dike raised barrier built to prevent or control flooding

"White Crane Ridge," or Baiheliang, is a 1,600-meter- (5,250-feet-) long and 25-meter- (82-foot-) wide smooth stone ridge. It is engraved with carvings about the Yangtze River. These date from 763 to the early 1900s. On the huge rock are 20 fish sculptures that serve as water-level markers. There are also about 30,000 characters of Chinese poems from different periods in history. It is said to be the world's oldest **hydrographic survey device**. Since it became part of the dam's reservoir, an underwater museum was built so people could still admire this work of art.

This photo shows a section of White Crane Ridge before it was swallowed by the reservoir.

Dam supporters claim that the level of protection given to **relics** in the Three Gorges Dam area has never been seen before in China. Of the 10,878 cultural sites listed, 723 were underground. Supporters say more scientific and technological tools than ever before were used to protect the relics. And according to a vice director of the State Administration of Cultural Heritage, the overall standard of protection being offered to the cultural relics of the Three Gorges area is first-rate.

It has also long been argued that the dam will bring jobs and an improved quality of life to tens of millions of people living in the interior of China. But time will judge the accuracy of claims like these.

From the beginning, many people have been vocal about potential problems with the Three Gorges Dam project. Now that the dam has been completed, it is becoming evident that there are problems with many of the arguments and claims made to support dam construction.

One of the many towns that was completely submerged by the reservoir.

Destruction and flooding

Thirteen major cities, 140 small cities and towns, 1,352 villages, 1,600 factories, and 700 schools were flooded by the reservoir. Many have disappeared completely. The city of Wanxian, with its major silk-weaving factories, was the largest victim. Two-thirds of the city was flooded.

Some people believe that the dam's flood-control benefits are exaggerated. They argue that the new reservoir can, at best, store only a fraction of the floodwaters entering the Yangtze River during a peak-flow year. There is also a contradiction between the dam's role in flood control and its hydroelectricity production. Flood control means keeping the reservoir water level low at certain times of the year. But hydroelectricity requires higher levels of water, to allow for the continual escape of water to produce electricity.

Pollution

Over one billion tons of wastewater go into the Yangtze River every year. As sewage travels downstream toward the dam, it collects waste as it goes. Chongqing and many other cities along the river flush tremendous amounts of sewage and toxic waste into the reservoir. The dam has slowed the Yangtze flow, reducing its ability to flush out waste. There is now more waste than the water can clean by itself. In addition, flooded buildings add to the pollution of the Yangtze.

In 2008 the State Environmental Policy Protection Administration (SEPA) of China stated that the water quality behind the Three Gorges Dam has not substantially improved, despite a plan to reduce pollution. Water quality is actually worsening in several branches of the Yangtze River that drain into the main reservoir.

Unfortunately, two-thirds of the dam's promised environmental projects have not yet been put into place. Under an updated plan, some 460 water-quality projects are set to begin during the next few years. The cost will possibly be higher than $3.2 billion. The water programs will help, but only if completed and monitored well.

Power problems

There is not enough electricity coming from the dam. China's power needs continue to grow as businesses expand and new cities are built. The dam was supposed to supply 10 percent of China's electricity. But with the country's rapidly growing economy, it may only produce 3 percent.

Silting and sedimentation

Flood fears persist because of sediment. The Yangtze, China's "Silt Road," is the fourth-largest sediment carrier in the world. Critics think the Yangtze's silt problem is getting worse, and say that the river will eventually add 530 million tons of silt to the reservoir every year.

In time this silt will accumulate behind the dam walls, clogging the **turbines**. This would reduce the dam's effectiveness in flood control. Critics also claim that the river will not flow fast enough to keep the turbines turning. Over time, the dam might become unable to operate. If sediment becomes thick enough, it might even cause the reservoir water to create a major waterfall by rising above the dam wall.

In addition, downstream regions will not get the fertile silt traditionally carried by the river, because the silt is trapped behind the dam.

Earthquakes and landslides

The Three Gorges Dam lies over a fault line. The dam is supposed to be able to withstand earthquakes. But the reservoir area also sees frequent mudflows and landslides. Underwater earthquakes and landslides can move enormous amounts of water. Huge waves of water could fall over the dam's top.

In 2007 officials and experts admitted that the project had caused many environmental problems. They warned that if preventative measures were not taken, it could lead to a major environmental disaster.

Chinese sturgeon are one of many species that have suffered because of the new dam.

Endangered animals

The Yangtze River is home to many water-dwelling animals. The Three Gorges Dam has increased river traffic, which has led to pollution, overfishing, slow-moving water, and the loss of many animal **habitats**. Water-dwelling animals have not been able to cope well with the drastic changes to the river.

WORD STORE   habitat a place where an animal naturally lives

In addition to losing about 80 varied food fish species, animals currently endangered on the Yangtze are the finless porpoise, Chinese sturgeon, Chinese alligator, and Siberian crane.

Cultural loss

During the construction of the dam, about 1,300 architectural sites were flooded. While some cultural and historical relics were moved, others could not be moved due to their location, size, or design.

FENGDU

Fengdu is the only "ghost town" in China. It contains 75 Buddhist and Taoist temples. The temples contained many statues. The Tao religion believes that when people die, their spirits will gather in Fengdu. In the spirit world, there are a series of super-beings in the temples. They all have their own responsibility, guarding the spirit world.

Located on the banks of the Yangtze, Fengdu was partially submerged by the Three Gorges Dam reservoir.

This photo shows Fengdu before the dam was completed. After the reservoir filled, the water level rose as high as the bridge.

45

POPULATION MOVEMENT

In 1990 the costs for the Three Gorges Dam were estimated at $12 billion. Estimates are that the final cost will reach $50 billion. This is more than any other single construction cost in history. However, about half of the costs have been from the resettlement of people near the dam construction zone.

An estimated 1.3 million people, perhaps as many as 2 million, were moved from the Three Gorges area as the dam was built. This cut them off from their roots and, for many, created devastating social instability. However, those living in cities near the Yangtze accepted the transfer with more enthusiasm than the **rural** residents.

The Chinese government built 13 new towns both inland and higher on the mountains. They constructed 2,260 kilometers (1,401 miles) of power transmission lines, plus 3,312 kilometers (2,053 miles) of telecommunication lines. The new cities offered new buildings and apartment houses with modern facilities, like indoor bathrooms. But these new homes were more expensive for residents than the wood, stone, or concrete-block homes they had left behind.

Relocating millions of people is a very difficult, and very controversial issue.

This is one of many new towns built to house the people who were relocated from the Three Gorges reservoir area.

Struggling to adapt

Many Yangtze city dwellers are still struggling to adapt to the changes brought about by the dam. However, those people previously employed by businesses were given a continued salary. Other newcomers opened small shops so that people could purchase items for their new homes. The new stores contained washing machines, flooring, wallpapers, curtains, and furniture. There was even advice offered on how to make a new home look pretty. There are new drugstores, hairdressers, restaurants, and tailors. Young people have adapted especially well. They have been pleased that the new schools have better equipment than their previous ones.

> **“** The rising reservoir has brought Wanzhou both great losses and great opportunities at the same time. **”**
>
> *Tan Hongbin, an official with the Wanzhou Resettlement Bureau*

But for the 400,000 rural people, who made their living from farming, the situation has been more difficult. Many families had been in their villages for generations. People married from their village or from a nearby village. Years of hard labor had transformed the land so that it would grow fruits, grain, and vegetables. This fed families and provided people with enough money to live on. The Chinese government knew it would be difficult to transfer peasants to other farmable land. But the transfer proved more difficult than they had expected.

The **reservoir** flooded about 30,300 hectares (75,000 acres) of the best farmland in the region. Resettled people who were able to continue farming had to do so on poorer-quality land than they had before. Many rural people, often poor to begin with, were moved to lands that weren't good for growing anything. But it was even more difficult for those who were transferred far from their original homes.

> **“** The environmental impacts of the project are profound [very serious], and are likely to get worse as time goes on. . . . Since 2007, Chinese scientists and government officials have become increasingly concerned about the environmental and social impacts of the project. **”**
>
> *from the environmental group International Rivers*

Some farmers volunteered to be transferred far away from the Three Gorges, in hopes of a better situation. They found not only different farming methods, but also neighbors who spoke a different dialect that they did not understand at all. Almost all of these volunteers returned to the Three Gorges area for relocation closer to their original homes. As necessary, the young and strong go out during the agricultural off-season to work as laborers in big cities.

Success or failure?

The Three Gorges Dam project is an amazing example of technology. Despite political setbacks and the pressure of having the entire world watching—and often criticizing—the dam arose. It functions. Does it function as expected? That depends on who is observing and commenting. There is no easy answer when dealing with science and human activity on such a huge scale. Only time will tell if the project was a major success or a disastrous failure.

" The Yangtze Gorge project. . . will be of utmost importance to China. It will bring great **industrial** developments in Central and Western China. It will bring widespread employment. It will bring high standards of living. It will change China from a weak to a strong nation. The Yangtze Gorge project should be constructed for the benefit of China and the world at large. "

from a report in 1944 by John Lucien Savage, a leading dam builder

THREE GORGES DAM STATS

The Three Gorges Dam wall is 185 meters (610 feet) high—as high as a 60-story building. It stretches 2.3 kilometers (1.4 miles) across the Yangtze River. The project required 463 tons of steel—enough to build 63 Eiffel Towers. It used 10.5 billion tons of cement.

About 60,000 workers were employed by the Three Gorges Dam project, with about 25,000 working on the dam itself. During construction, about 100 workers died in accidents.

TIMELINE OF THE THREE GORGES DAM PROJECT

1919 Sun Yat-sen proposes a flood-control dam for the Three Gorges area. Due to political and economic problems, the dam idea does not progress.

1931 The Yangtze River causes a major flood.

1935 The Yangtze River causes a major flood.

1953 Chairman Mao Zedong first proposes a flood-control dam for the Three Gorges area.

1954 The Yangtze River causes a major flood.

1970 The Gezhouba Dam is proposed as an alternate to the Three Gorges Dam.

1988 The Gezhouba Dam is completed, but is not a satisfactory alternative.

1990 Premier Li Peng insists on a review of the Three Gorges Dam project.

1992 The Chinese government votes on the Three Gorges Dam project.

1993 Construction teams enter the dam site for the first time.

1993–1997 Stage one of construction gets underway on the Three Gorges Dam. This includes earthmoving, the completion of cofferdams, the damming of the Yangtze River, and construction of the vertical ship lift. The diversion channel opens, and ships begin traveling through it. The expressway from Yichang to the dam site, and Xiling Bridge across the Yangtze, are open to traffic.

1998 The Yangtze River causes a major flood.

1998–2003 Stage two of construction gets underway. This includes completion of the dam's spillway, completion of the left bank powerhouse, and continued construction of the permanent ship lock system. The first two turbine generators begin producing power.

2003–2008 All 26 electricity-producing turbines are completed. The last cofferdam is destroyed. The five-story permanent ship lock begins full operation. Reservoir water depth is 175 meters (574 feet).

GLOSSARY

capacity the total amount that something can contain

cofferdam temporary watertight walls used in construction projects in areas that are normally underwater

dike raised barrier built to prevent or control flooding

diversion channel area where river waters are redirected while a dam is built

drought a shortage of water caused by unusually low rainfall

erosion wearing away of soil or rock by water or other forces of nature

generator very large electric motor containing magnets and wires. Generators are used to turn mechanical energy into electrical energy.

habitat the place where an animal naturally lives

hydroelectric electric current produced by the energy of moving water

hydrographic survey device a scientific device used for measuring, charting, or describing a body of water

industrial having to do with industries. Industries are businesses that are usually based around processing raw materials and making goods in factories.

industrialization the process of developing industries

kilowatt unit of power equal to 1,000 watts. A typical household incandescent lightbulb uses electrical energy at a rate of 25 to 100 watts.

lock system similar to an enormous elevator that works in shifts. Locks are used to move boats up or down by raising or lowering water levels

National People's Congress (NPC) one of the three main areas of power in China's government. The other two are the State Council and the president.

premier the premier is the head of the State Council, one of the three main areas of power in China's government. The other two are the NPC and the president.

relic the remains of an object from an earlier time

remote far-off

reservoir place where water is collected and stored for use

rural country

sediment particles that drop to the bottom of water or other liquid

sewage wastewater

silt deposit of mud or fine soil from moving water

sluice human-made channel for conducting water with a valve or gate to regulate the flow

State Council one of the three main areas of power in China's government. The other two are the NPC and the president. The premier is the head of the State Council.

turbine propeller-like piece of equipment, which turns a metal shaft in an electric generator

FIND OUT MORE

BOOKS

Barter, James. *The Yangtze*. San Diego: Lucent, 2003.

Behnke, Alison. *China in Pictures*. Minneapolis, MN: Lerner, 2003.

Bowden, Rob. *The Yangtze*. Chicago: Raintree, 2004.

Fredericks, Carrie, ed. *Water*. Detroit: Greenhaven, 2006.

Gay, Kathlyn. *Mao Zedong's China*. Minneapolis, MN: Twenty-First Century, 2008.

Hansen, Amy S. *Hydropower: Making a Splash!* New York: PowerKids, 2010.

Mah, Adeline Yen. *China: Land of Dragons and Emperors*. New York: Delacorte, 2008.

Petersen, Christine. *Water Power*. New York: Children's Press, 2004.

Sebag-Montefiore, Poppy. *Eyewitness: Modern China*. New York: DK Eyewitness, 2007.

Stewart, Whitney. *Mao Zedong*. Minneapolis, MN: Twenty-First Century, 2006.

Streissguth, Thomas. *China in the 21st Century: A New World Power*. Berkeley Heights, NJ: Enslow, 2008.

Uschan, Michael V. *China Since World War II*. Detroit: Lucent, 2008.

WEBSITES

Water Use: Hydroelectric Power
http://ga.water.usgs.gov/edu/wuhy.html
This site has a discussion of hydropower worldwide, and its advantages and disadvantages.

Hydroelectric Power: How It Works
http://ga.water.usgs.gov/edu/hyhowworks.html
This site discusses how we get electricity from water.

TVA Kids: Hydroelectric Power
www.tvakids.com/electricity/hydro.htm
This site has more in-depth discussions of hydropower, and some information on other kinds of power plants.

Great Wall Across the Yangtze: Three Gorges Dam
www.pbs.org/itvs/greatwall/dam.html
This site has a discussion of the dam's history, Mao Zedong's involvement, and further discussion on the dam's pros and cons.

Exploring Chinese History: Special Report: The Three Gorges Dam Project
www.ibiblio.org/chinesehistory/contents/07spe/specrep01.html
This site has an in-depth article that examines some of the economic, environmental, social, and political impacts of the dam.

TOPICS TO LEARN MORE ABOUT

- **The Communist Party of China**
  Research the Chinese system of government and find out how projects like the Three Gorges Dam are dealt with.

- **Hydroelectric power and other renewable energy sources**
  Is hydroelectric power the best option for countries as they try to move away from "dirty" energy sources like coal? Research other renewable energy options, such as solar, wind, and geothermal power, to see what the pros and cons are for each.

INDEX

Franklin Pierce University

00198840

DATE DUE